What's There to See

Poetry, Life, Awakening, Satire, AI, Politics

By Jonnie Wall

Copyright © 2024 Janice C. Wall

All rights reserved.

No portion of this book may be reproduced in any form without written permission from the author, except as permitted by U.S. copyright law.

ISBN: 9798874213084

Introduction

Confusion in class, has been brought to attention

What does Lovie mean, the glossary doesn't mention

Lovie is a term, nothing more nothing less

Used for those who somehow feel blessed

Blessed enough to share, always with a smile

Willing to stand strong, willing to sit in exile

Just be kind, easy enough thing to do

Leave people wondering what, when your thru

Lovies get we are different, but really the same

Social differences being different, same game

Almost there class, good question, let's start again

Back to confusion, always a good place to begin

Contents

Welcome	1
Choices	3
Been Said Been Told	6
Demons	8
Chained Early	10
Mass Awakening	13
Home	15
Change of Season	18
Inside out	20
Tasks	22
Do It Now	24
Phones Up	26
Accommodation	27
Computer Stress	29
Tech Genius	30
Building a Future	32
Rainbow	34
1900 Feminist	36
Modern Day Feminist	37
Warrior	39
Queen of my Domaine	42
Gentlemen	44
Windy words	46
Religion	48
Offended	50
Toilet lid	51
Burn No Bridges	52
Ties	54
Children	56
Military Mom	58
US Military	59
Future History	60
Taxes	62
War and the Economy	64
Red Rhino	66
Balance broken	68
Passive Aggressive	69
X'ers grandparents	70
Narcissus Empathy	72
Madness	74
History	76
Pay The Cost	77
Negative?	78
Medical	79
Salesman	81
Look Away Part?	82
Excellence	84
Sexual Revolution	86
Free Energy	88
Too Much Noise	90
Not enough Time	91
No more Fun	92
Fight Flight	93
Living Yin Yang	94
Big I little i	96
Till we meet again	98
About Me	100

Welcome

Oh good, you came back

Been accused of little tact

Opening page, things are about to get blunt

Come now Lovies, dig in, save the grunt

Moving on from Diddly do to Diddly de

Diddle de, Diddle do, what's more to see

Might get bumpy, always done with love

Sometimes the problem lies in using kid gloves

Feeling the positive, bigger fish to fry

Humanity stuff, look away before you cry

Strong make weak, weak become strong or meek

History continues, just another week

Meek lash out nowhere to turn

What happened, what have we learned

Media lies at every turn

They'll tell you this, they'll tell you that

War, they don't give a crap

Turn off, by turning in, dig deep, this is only 101

You'll feel more confident when it's done

Seeing the dark side is easy

Diddly is light and kind of cheesy

Find the diddly in the des to come

Warriors spread peace, love and of course fun

Choices

Likes, dislikes, first step on a child's first path

Leaning confidence, making choices, reading or math

Force feed them peas or let them decide

Holy crap, parenthood is a ride

Time to sit, no wait, too small

Crawling, walking, slow down, don't fall

Don't forget those delicious peas

Pass the peas please, y'all know what that means

Somethings you do with a smile on your face

Somethings are done, just for grace

Learn to eat peas, to be polite

Not everything needs to be a fight

Likes, dislikes change, some stay the same

Smiling with grace, always win the game

Back to those Pea's, maybe Q's

Old folk lore, get confused

Basically saying, early limits, later reward

Left unchecked, welcome discord

Break that spirit it must be done

Ever watch a horse break, kind of fun

Nothing useful if it can't behave

Progressed to the point back in the cave

Too many babies not learning to eat peas

Plenty of veggies not so much please

Great, let children have their voice

Great to letting them have a choice

Someone must step in at some point

Maybe not, could end up in the joint

Joint, as in jail, words change as much as likes

Waiting to see what comes from next gens tikes

Been Said Been Told

Been said, been told, man is born with evil in his soul

What if said man is good even if greed is the goal

Gaze at an infant new to this life, try to find bad in those eyes

Screams like a hellion, whimpers and cries

Life has begun, heart filled with joy, nothing can compete

First thing learned, demand, demand something to eat

The greed to eat or the drive to survive

Evil little scamper, demanding to thrive

So innocent, so sweet, so pure

Pinch those cheeks, an angel for sure

Greedy at birth, instinct to survive

Survival, greedy, somewhere there's a lie

First words spoken, learned from others

Spiritual, academic, fathers and mothers

Evil is evil all else is not

Sit down, shut up, evil snot

Light in the dark, dark in the light

Same words different shades, wrong vs. right

Life passes, adventure, success, failure, maybe more

Childlike wonder, peeking around every corner, every door

Born or made, creation or create, who can say

Different ways of looking at thing a different way

Night searching for day, day holding back night

The battle for man's soul rages on eternal fight

Peace Love and Happiness a daily plight

Demons

Face your fear, set yourself free

Be everything you are meant to be

Look deep, find the cause

That little demon, the one that makes you pause

Always there, ready for adventure, maybe a dare

Harmless prankster, mother beware

Those over there, have demons bigger most

Greed demons, grifters out to coast

It's a game of chance, which way to play

Risk it all, save it for another day

Shiny new car or save for a home

Gotta have some time to roam

Which gets your attention, demon fun

Not enough time in the day to get it all done

Work all day, saving, hoping for more

Scary, Scary, what a bore

2 little demons, still there's more

Fear demon, scariest for sure

Fear, makes you do things you normally wouldn't

Fear is different than shouldn't

Irrational and driven, scary pair

Timid and frightened where to go from there

Demon number 3, 4 I'm sure there's more

Conquer fear, even out the score

Chained Early

Free spirit anchored soul

Somewhere between lies a hole

Anchored or tied not sure which way to go

No worries, got time, taking it slow

Don't stray too far from home

Untether free to roam

2020 stripped roaming away

Told not to play, roam, what to say

Free spirit anchored soul

Anchored spirit shackled goal

Free spirit no anchor, run away

Ties that bind a thing of yesterday

No thought of others, consequences may come

Run along free spirit, have some fun

2020, stripped day to day

Told not to play, roam, what to say

The spirit shackled before it could grow

Better for society or a major blow

Shackle children, the freest of free

Slow down progress, decide who they should be

Happened quickly, some got hit harder than others
Depended on fate, chance, media covers
Small group of children will only know what and why
Future is coming, hoping for laughter not a cry
Happened quickly, some got hit hard, some just coast
Depended on fate, looking back, hard to boast
Free spirit let lose, after the cage
Joyful, helpful, caring or full of rage
History will tell us what comes next
Gotta run, Granddaughter just sent a text

Mass Awakening

Mass awakenings happen year after year
Change, always somewhat of a fear
Winter hits, weather does what weather does
Buckles up, there might be a fuss
Tumble, stumble, adapt or hide
Mother Nature sure delivers a ride
Spring sets in, the awaking begins
Everyone out with smiles and grins
Checkers seem friendlier, gone is the freeze
Is it chaos, or peace felt in the breeze
Spring prepares for summer, we all know what that means
Summer specials, only the heat can bring
Out and about, scurrying thru the sunshine day
Summertime laughter, what more is there to say
Forgotten quickly the winter haze
Those who struggled through, stand in amaze
Quickly forgotten, how close the flood had come
Back last winter, fingers, toes and nose got numb
Open the doors, pass the plate around

No where to look, no help to be found

Back to summer, winter has past

Looking back, winter may have been a blast

The heat is heating up, shade is hard to find

Water is getting scarce, don't get left behind

Where did all this clutter come from, it suddenly appeared

Left over from winter, thought it got cleared

Stepping over what's left as it continues to grow

Springs awaking fading, losing its glow

The awaking continues until it stops

Soon petals will begin to drop

Dropped seeds scattered, ready to bloom

Mass awaking around the corner, coming soon

Home

Home or house a place to hang your hat

A place gathering dust or more than that

A house full of love a house full of plants

Joyfully playing, crazy times filled with rants

Your story starts in the home you were raised

House of horrors, home filled with praise

We don't get to choose the hand we are dealt

Two eyes locked, two hearts melt

Time to delve in, things to see

Hard to look, easier to turn on the TV

Signs all around, not even hard to miss

Drive by long enough, easy to dismiss

Tents now days, kids sleeping under the stars

Crazy times, talk of going to mars

No real answers just a lot of guess

No God, maybe, look at the mess

Too much interface or enough for the times

Money, kids, house is a mess, here's a dime

Maybe it can be fixed maybe it can't

"Look away" dropped line to diddly do rant

So much to do, the pandemic took its toll

It's ok, here, hug this doll

Those working are working hard, they can't do it all

Get straight with God, time to stand tall

The Gov won't save you, they've shown they won't

Hard times ahead, please God don't

Building a home from a house takes time

What, thought it happened at the drop of a dime

A house you see from the outside nothing more

Home is what you get when you step in the door

Drive by, stop or look away

Crazy times, awaking type of day

Change of Season

Spring is here, end of March twenty-three

Excited to see what changes soon will be seen

Rough couple of years, draughts, floods, record snow

Seasons are off, maybe not, back on track more to go

Someone's messing with the weather, only mother nature knows

Remember back, spring sprung twice this year

Berries bloomed early, late snow being a fear

Noticed a few small differences, nothing to big

More broken branches, twisted up twigs

Rough winter, weeding out the grass from the moss

Lost some good ones, weathering the storm, has its cost

Mid-April last big push of winter in the air

Spring is here, really, you can feel it near

Blossoms are blooming, birds are nesting nearby

Spring is here, clean out the clutter, time to fly

Summer started early, got dry and hot here

Living in a rain forest, dry is a fear

Fall hit late, hot summer, paid the price

Cooler temperatures, vibrant colors, feels kind of nice

Winter is near, so much going down

Twenty-three, tough season all around

Inside out

Humans worked hard sheltering from the storm

Who would have thought, inside would become the norm

Dirty windows tint out vitamin D, y'all know, the sunrays

That little thing that somehow lightens the day

Pollution is polluting the air they say

Stay safe use this blocker, stop the sun

Initial panic will subside, you'll be glad when it's done

Adjust the lights, create an atmosphere

Outside lingers, sun and wind, will the mind clear

Pipe in music, calm the nerves

Check out the delivery, nice curves

Outside, sun, light, lighter load

Crawling insects, frog, or toad

Finding a balance between too much of both

Too much of anything stunts human growth

Build tunnels, connect town to town

Buy up forest, shut them down

Yards are too big, need more space

We just keep getting bigger, the human race

Run on a treadmill, sweat while going nowhere

It is better than nothing to be honestly fair

Inside out, outside in

Now where to go not sure where to begin

Tasks

9 months hard labor, 3 to rest

Some say 5 would be best

What we have now never ends

Morning starts, night day blend

Tasks keep time on the clock

Lunch time, great spot around the block

Need an appointment, break the busy day

Losing time, task master has the say

Next task on the list must get done

Tasks, wasted time, money to some

Tasks never end, task the day you sign up

Sit down, relax, have a soothing cup

Do It Now

This needs to be done, liceity quick

Not too fast, could be a trick

Do it now or be left behind

Sitting back watching, almost a crime

No time to think just react

Slow down now, getting off track

What must be done now, really must

Now, drop everything or miss the bus

Do it Now, nothing else matters

Life or death, spilled milk, life shatters

Do it Now needs to maybe relax

React, react based on who's facts

Do it now, think it thru

Do what and when you need to

Pressure changes every day

Stay the course, Now, when you say

Phones Up

Scamper on isle three, parents' text in

Phones down parents, a place to begin

You don't do it, you know you do

Text in complaints, boo, hooo

Sure, scamper is fine on isles three

Sorry for the poor soul kicked in the knee

Scamper needs attention, phone, not the place

We all do it, check the mirror, check the face

Complaining about the kiddo's trying to survive

Phone beeps, must check, maybe something to hide

Caught up in the moment forgetting about today

Better keep up, competition is the best way

Compete to win no matter the cost

Scamper on isle 3 sadly still lost

All on alert phones beeping everywhere

Come get your scamper, the crowd angrily glares

Accommodation

Accommodating, virtue or vice

Neither none, better check twice

Accommodating, giving shelter and love

Spreading Peace, Love, release the white dove

Accommodating sacrificing, what more to give

Somewhere in the middle most hopefully live

Some go so far that it becomes their life

Gifting others comfort easing their strive

Come drop by for a visit, stay the day

Stay to long, get the stick, shew away

Accommodating accommodating, what a chore

Getting dark, thinking back, striving for more

Circle continues, giver or taker of the coin

Accommodations here, sign up, sign in, join

Getting crowded, raise the price to attend

Collect, collection a good place to begin

Overextended the accommodator is worn out

Virtue left wounded vice becomes a pout

Diddle De Notes

Computer Stress

They call it computer stress, give suggestion

It's you not the computer, says the above mentioned

Computer stress, how to beat it and why

Computer people are strange, Wi-Fi keeps them tied

Always about the screen, underneath the real fun

Live in the digital world, easier to sit back than run

If you don't do computers, then what do you do

Computer life's the way, when will that get through

Life spins by, tech has it all figured out

The sun is shining, pull the shades, it'll make you doubt

Computer on, first thing in the morn

Off at night or else you might not have been born

Kids know computers from the very start

Conveniently hid, inside a plastic toy heart

Will computer stress in time fade away

It's just another part of kids' day today

Tech Genius

Tech help is needed in every home

Not just tech tech, how about that phone

TV remotes, receivers too

Tech help is needed, do not know what to do

Booming business, can you stay on the line

No problem, it's not yet my dime

Can I help you, what's you're beef

This happened, life of its own, good grief

Slow down, let me walk you thru a few steps

Reps on the way just in case, place your bets

All squared away back to norm

Tech genius in every dorm

Some just don't get it, it's not that hard

Open deck, shuffle, pick a card

Sleight of hand, fingers now days

Technology changed magic in mysterious ways

Get from point B to point D with click

Technology, magic, another trick

Building a Future

Are you a wait and see or get it done

Scratching at scabs never fun

The future is yours, it's in your hand

Scour the woods, scrub off the land

Follow the rules even if they change

Here comes a shift, time to rearrange

Pushing pushing, only way forward

Out of the way you coward

Look at that castle, no look straight ahead

Finish line awaits it's all in your head

Believing you will win without the cost

Somewhere along the way something got lost

Build a world that represents you

Time will tell what good you do

Something spectacular, something small

Quiet, secluded, extravagant, have a ball

Build the life you want to live

Work for it, remember to give

Pieces will begin to fall into place

Remember, God's loving grace

Rainbow

Peace, Love, Happiness, the highest goal

Easier to look outside, inside holds the soul

Colors of the rainbow, symbol of hope

A sign, a warning, a, I told you so

The earth was flooded, how much, when, who knows

Books out there with dates made into shows

A reminder that after the rain, comes the sun

A sign of aftermath, look what's been done

Rainbows have always been there, a prism of the sun

Run along, grab some paint, have some fun

Red, yellow, green, colors on down from there

The colors are pretty, the order, don't care

It's the magic of the colors splitting up the rain

Gloomy and bright produce a color train

Rainbows are for everyone, everyone agrees

Merchandise made a fortune, remember, greed

Peace, Love and Happiness, what a goal

Gotta dig deep, somewhere in your soul

The sun is gloomy, clouds have full display

Praying soon the rainbows will chase the gloom away

The weather today, dry, when it should be rain

God's hiding his rainbow, man's is on full display

The arc is swinging, how much will be lost

Distorting God's rainbow, comes with a cost

A few stragglers will continue most will slip away

Too much too soon, the masses said, not today

1900 Feminist

Early 1900's great grandmother stood tall

Strong, young, beautiful, had it all

A feminist they called her, she wanted more

It burned inside her, she wanted her own store

Women owning business, back then, not so much

Grandpa was there to help, pretty solid hunch

Stories of debt collectors, start-ups shutting down

Great grandma was not unknown around town

Nanna I called her, story time and apples on her lap

Listened while she read, maybe thinking I was taking a nap

She read the classics, she read them out loud

Dante, Homer, Plato, old Harvard crowd

The classics passed down, at first, not sure why

Adult realization, great grandmothers' gift, wings to fly

Cost me points along the way

Without knowing, I always had something, smart, to say

Where do her stories come from, why such big thoughts

Nanna's stories of the past, much better gift than store bought

7 generations should know, who you are

Nanna would say looking up at the Stars

You are lucky, 3 are already known to you

The other 4, depend on the good you do

The new Harvard crowd has changed, time and time again

Academia following, the biggest and newest trend

Those old classics sit on my shelf, a reminder of time

Classics remain, look around, the best are easiest to find

Modern Day Feminist

Y'all minions she said with a crown on her head

Listen up, listen up you people I dread

What's best for me is what's best for all

Here for the little people, big and small

Send me your tokens, more than a dime

Cells are awaiting, cover up that crimes

Under the table, above the crowd

Dazzling, elegant, a fabulous wow

Get to work girls there is more to do

Remember bend and drop, now tie your shoe

Bring them down one by one

Shredding little men, always fun

Cackly old lady can barely stand on her feet

Gather around crowd she's passing out treats

Come on ladies is this really our best

Modern day feminist, what a mess

Warrior

Warriors have flaws, without, there'd be no cause

Questioning questions, requesting a pause

Warriors recognizes danger while the masses sing

Open your mind, fight for life, define life, confusion, see what it brings

Life, that thing we are living each day

Life, who has what, who has the say

Look in the eye of a pet, wildlife better yet

Gifts to man, lesser form, roll of the dice, wagers bet

Do they see our society as busy ants, granted, luxury pants

It all ties together, promise, ignore the rants

The more nature grows, the more man says stop

Man, well, he needs somewhere to shop

Beyond heartbeat in nature, is a kill

Don't know the difference, definitely not on the same pill

Back to the pets, birds, wildlife held dear

What must they think, gaining trust or fear

We forget they've been watching, who knows what they think

Their struggle is for life, man flushes it away in a blink

Where is the profit to man, to see life this way

Here for now, only one way, only one say

Which life gets to be heard, define it I dare

To complicating, not enough data or really don't care

Are we really that species that cares only about us

Good food, cheap wine no drama no fuss

What's good for the gander, not always good for the goose

The gander gets grander the goose just loose

Flapping around, ties unseen

The joy of life, the joy of all living things

Lost in self, all the sparkly things

No time for distractions discards the unwanted glob

Planned parenthood doing its job

Warrior's warning, drive by, throw trash and insults

Societies looks away, present day result

Gone too far, no one can tell why or how

Breakdown of family, community, lost in the now

Back to those pesty wildlife, living natures life

Man is different, man gets to choose, confusion causes strife

This path leads here, that trail there

Wander around a tad, you'll get somewhere

Generations lost stumbling, warriors stand strong

Lifting up the broken, standing for life, pushing back wrong

Warriors stand strong, knowing the fight for life is right

Warriors fight for more than now, they fight for life's light

Queen of my Domaine

It takes a strong Women to iron out a man

Wear the pants, stay at home or not a fan

Wear a dress, party all night

Iron away in the morning what a fright

Ok to lead or stay behind

There's more to option 2 you'll fined

It's a tad bit freeing working only for 2

Got a bit harder when the crew grew

Ties that tie what incredible thoughts

Ties that can and will never be bought

Behind a strong man is a Women willing to give her all

They've always had one, since they were small

They carry themselves differently, knowing they are not alone

The king and the queen, together on their throne

King/Queen of my Domaine was once said to me

Took it too heart, isn't that what freedom means

Ruler of my Domaine, yes, it is very small

The branches branch out, it's getting tall

The trunk is willowy, sturdy, swaying in the breeze

Branches grow up and out, study shelter, for nature's needs

2 together make a stronger force

Slows you down a bit when changing course

You can tell who's a Queen with a King by her side

Mingling smiles, chatty talk, beaming with pride

Queen with a King type always stands out

Confidence to make even the doubters doubt

Gentlemen

The Gentleman, he's out there, hard to find

Gentle man, tough, successful, helpful, mostly kind

You just feel safe when he's about

Most men now days, stand back and pout

Stood tall, mask, no mask, everyone's a friend

No hand-outs, no glopping newest trends

Pre-Covid, subtle difference became a glaring thing

Subtle misdirection, only passing time brings

Gentlemen wink, others stare you down

Reaching for the top shelf, not a gentleman to be found

Reaching overhead, a hand misplaced

Gentlemen reaches first, applause erupts in the place

Feat was simply just getting some sauce

Without the gentleman, could've been a lost cause

The crowd like watching, the gentleman made it two

Gentlemen don't watch, they know what to do

Stranded among strangers putting on a show

Hoping for a gentlemen to soften the blow

Windy words

Words flew by without a care

Branches, limbs flying in the air

Wind whines down nothing to say

Just another turbulent day

Gust come from nowhere

Leaving debris without any care

Words in the wind tossed as a dare

Breezy, playful, windy day

Blustery, stormy, either way

Words without care, heavy or lite

Words of praise, words of spit

Wind blows past so do words

Disrupted balance, broken wounds

Religion

A diddly about religion, did she just go there

Religion, everything we hold common, rarely share

This way or that, pay your dues join the cause

Forgetting to slow down, take a pause

Pause you must not, there is work to get thru

Better skedaddle somewhere else, pressing things to do

Religion is busy, look around can you see

Religion is more, religion is us, it's diddly de

Is your religion ridged, relaxed, get the cue

Not wrong or bad, it's comfortable for you

Pull back the curtain, peek behind the scenes

Strange diddly, who knows what it means

So many religions, all kinds, sort of mean the same thing

Religion gives the soul a voice to sing

God the Creator loved his children, he set us Free

Here on earth, struggles, to be all we can be

The Creator created his creation whatever the creators name

Some have differences, yet all kind of the same

Who's to blame the blame on, the blamer game

Who's taking the credit, who's hiding in shame

Religion, corner stone of life, deny, except, it's all the same

Offended

Stop being offended vs. offensive, never gave it much thought

Stay quick, be submissive, is what was taught

Same today, just in different ways

Offence to the senses, nod ok

Question the chaos, pay the price

Do as told, do not play nice

It's ok, no bother who laughs when or why

Diddly of confusion, did I make you cry

Gone are the days of jokingly poking fun

Crossed lines, not needed, blocked the sun

Granted, it most likely went too far

Everyone now day has to be the star

Have to say no if you want your way

Say no first give other no room to say

Offensive behavior has become the norm

Go shopping, whip up a storm

Stand up to offensive, offended "they" be

You're stepping out of line, now do you see

The circle continues until one steps up or steps away

The bickering only ends when, maybe another day

Toilet lid

A rainbow on a toilet lid can only mean one thing

Light reflecting through the window, can you hear the birds sing

Light through the window, hitting a mirror

Songbirds vocal, the rainbow appears

Such an odd sight, shut the lid and flush

It's just a rainbow why such a fuss

Twisted mother nature through the window pane

Rainbow on a toilet lid, surely insane

Agree, what a wonder such a great sign

Act of God, manmade, by design

Burn No Bridges

Burn no bridge was told the other day

What an odd thought to say

A bridge has 2 sides, twice the burn

Give and take, always a turn

Thoughts will linger good or bad

Turn away, open arms, happy or mad

Test the waters still smoldering on one side

Smiles waiting arms opened wide

Burn no bridges, as if it could be done by one

Burning bridges, walk away what's done is done

Awkward meeting, stolen glance

One sided, betting chance

Bridge between friends or a passing nod

Too many bridges watering down the cause

Bridges that are sturdy take more than heat

Sturdy takes a pounding ready for the next beat

Burn no bridges, what a thought

Cross on over saved you a spot

Ties

Ties that bind or do they hold

Ties that free allowing to be bold

Ties that bind, someone else's toy

Ties that allow for growth and joy

Ties that tie never giving in

Ties that release letting good begin

Ties around your neck, around your wrist

Ties tiedown, double up that fist

Freedom to wander knowing ties are there

Broken ties, left with despair

Tie that tie, are they your own

Wings to fly when you have grown

Tie must be broken always ask why

Tie that tie, reaching for the sky

Children

Raising children, hardest thing to do

Changing diapers, picking up doggie poo

Needy, the same depending on who you ask

Run along, interrupting a task

Full grown at 2 no longer a pup

Scamper, takes so long to grow up

Differences noted, back to the task at hand

Toddlers can be challenging, spectator fan

Elementary years slip by, try to keep up

By Middle, they'll run in, what's for sup

Buy a car, you know you must

Pull back on that leash or so you trust

Getting close to the edge, let go or pull in

Parenting on over drive, open road begins

Welcome to children, we've all been one

Remember back, remember the fun

What goes around comes around so they say

Children, the grandest part of the day

Diddle De Notes

Military Mom

Military mom, what a thing to be

Action, glamor, all there is to see

Peace is great, advance, learn and grow

War? War is something very few know

Military parent, during Covid, strange indeed

Fenced capital, armed guards, what did it mean

Military under attack, there and at home

Talk about amazon deliveries by drone

Real world and military world, collide by divide

One step out of military, what a ride

Pray for our Warriors, they really do fight for right

US military fights for Freedom, Freedom is worth the fight

US Military

US military, one of a kind, volunteers paid with taxpayers dimes

Volunteer to protect the US citizens from worldly crimes

Forgotten unless reminded, the price for most too high

Taxpayers complain about expenses until the shit hits the sky

Not enough volunteers for the crimes of the world

Sign up for the draft, numbers are low boys and girls

Hitting close to home, why did they look away

Crimes continue, for military, just another day

Homelessly scattered, too much to fast

Looking through windows searching a lost past

Stand tall thru the storm, the battle continues on

US Military, protecting US, dusk till dawn

Future History

How will history look back on this time

Today, even mentioning Covid is a crime

Hostile takeovers left and right

Politics, religion, people no will to fight

Broken and beaten hanging by a thread

Celebrating history or everyday a dread

Can not escape it, the virus continues to spread

Run along gas is expensive bury your head

A country that has always had more than enough

More for some, less for other, some, downright tough

Debt keeps building, spending keeps up, taxes soared

Angry generation left pounding on the door

War is back in the headlines, it was quiet for a time

Spending, spending, who wants the taxpayers dime

Not yet '24, still more to see

Will history remember Covid, what will be, will be

Taxes

Taxes you say, it's time to vote

Taxing so fast going to go broke

Taxes on services, goods and land

Half what is made goes to the man

Take before the check even gets cashed

Under the table makes transactions fast

Tax, ok if what is needed is done

Nothing fixed, need more tax, glare from the sun

Voters are smarter or maybe not

Maybe they like the system they got

A lot of complaining, nothing done, taxes go up

Crooked dealings, maybe a broken water pump

Vote how you like, hope you're not a pawn

Government and taxes, don't water your lawn

Pay your taxes, look away, let the Government do

Remember, the tax vote came from you

War and the Economy

War is helpful to the economy, we learned during WW2

Gives the masses something to focus on, productive things to do

Without war, haven't been there for some time

Nothing big here, just pull out the purse, produced a dime

The economy afforded me this big purse of mine

It's rare, unique, expensive, quite a find

If the war machine stopped, what would happen to me

Big purse, remember greed

Hopelessly lost between War and Peace

Never step foot in battle, what a relief

Greed, war, taxes, the roundabout continues

Middle will decide, hope that doesn't offend you

The 60's came and the 60's went

Long time ago, Peace and Love kind of bent

Leaders are leading they say, they know best

Stand strong, slave to greed, ultimate test!

Same leaders today as before

60's Peace, Love, Money, revolving door

Red Rhino

Red Rhino, Blue Mule, middle voter follow the rules

War and Economy, establishment tools

It's all about the economy, told time and time again

Back to War, how about No, let's find a new trend

A short 4-year glimpse of how it could be

Gas dropped along with taxes, not enough time to see

Things started getting fuzzy, sometime after three

Red Rhino, Blue Mule, hide when it starts to get tough

Social, trendy, fluffy kind of stuff

Economy/War slogan is losing its appeal

The middle is shrinking, war economy, a losing deal

Red Rhino, Blue Mule will have to decide

How much, how soon are you prepared for the ride

War has been good to the middle these past years

It's over there, business booming, economy strong here

Can the middle envision an economy without war

Not here, over there, on their shore

Red Rhino's decide, Blue Mule take the dare

Establishments tools, middle will pay the fare

Balance broken

Offensive, defensive, no middle, balance not seen

Swaying side to side no stillness in between

Raging forward or shrinking back

Day to day living, under attack

Wired, taught, made that way

Offensive, defensive not a word to say

Screamed at as a child, parents under stress

Offensive defensive, child's first test

Off balance early, stable gets harder to find

Stressed out and stressed, no time to unwind

Vacation they say escape from your day

Balance will still be broken fix you ways

Running thru straight ahead no end in sight

Offensive, defensive, off balance ready to fight

Passive Aggressive

Passive aggressive, aggressive passive, different but the same

Push retreat, retreat attack, it all depends on your game

Passive until not, attacks when pushed too far

Aggressive, ready with an apology, sorry about the scar

Aggressive is the way, nothing holding you back

Disagree, better have something heavy in that sack

Agree, agree, agree, let the wars wager on

Silly hippies, peace and love, until something goes wrong

Poke the passive it's kind of fun

Better run like shit when you are done

Passive aggressive, small, fuming mad

The best kind of target an aggressor can have

X'ers grandparents

X'er grandparents, you're out there you know you are

Watching babies, raising babies, tikes never too far

In our 20's real life hit us full in the face

Everyone running, going, competing, frantic pace

Some were old, some were young, all had kids the same age

Different time of life, divergent page

Easy to sit back now watch and smile

Our babies' babies walking that first mile

The masked generation, silently speaking out

Stepping in stepping up, maybe a little doubt

Our grandchildren watched as pretty much, everyone fought

Peace, love, the battle cry we all taught

Some looked on, fear behind their eyes

Others pushed back, stood tall, silenced their cries

Wipe those tears, here, have a fresh apple slice

Not for the kiddo but for our kids

Some of you did great, others, first thing, hid

Where you a active grandparent during the flu

Boomers I get, but X'ers, what about you

Watching our babies carry the burden of raising tike

New territory for the books, research, grants, tax hikes

Our grandkids will remember most what we did

Getting late, calling a Lid

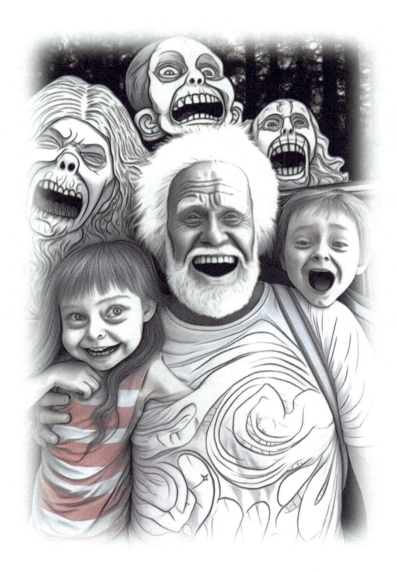

Narcissus Empathy

Narcissus and Goldmund, 1930, Hesse, what a book

Digs inside every flaw, every strength, crannies and nooks

Not sure you've heard of it, really, why

Empathy on full display, narcists comply

One hundred years ago or suddenly found

Hidden beneath clutter, buried in the ground

Linked to this or link to that

Might be linked to, oh dang, drat

Easily dismissed, hidden out of sight

Narcissus and Goldmund, might have got it right

Can you mention a book written so long ago

Or will, the powers of be say no

Any who class, still a good read

Off to make dinner, it's time to feed

Madness

Have you entered into madness

The low the high the euphoria the sadness

Madness that follows, years it takes

Personal madness, not crazy, not fake

Maybe madness because of mad

Madness because of sad

Broken bottles of madness scattered what a mess

The final battle of darkness the first or final test

Madness released, bubbly brew brought to a simmer

Darkness lifting, light starting to shimmer

Madness restored, will once again contained

Personal growth madness restrained

History

History written history past

History forgotten, somethings just pass

Mini me must be something more

Teach me teach me something pure

Pure white, pure black either way

Stuck in the middle with nothing to say

Learn from mistakes, pass them on

History forgotten, boom they are gone

Mistakes repeated, only to be faced again

History can be and is a friend

Others teach while those who do hold back

History being passed down, on a broken track

No one knows your history better than you

No ones history is the same, getting a clue

History is generational, made and taught

History lost, paid for and bought

A member of the human race

Surely your history has a place

Generations continue throughout the ages

History written, history saved in the pages

Pay The Cost

Get a degree they say, legitimize who you are

Doesn't matter what it's in, it'll make you better by far

A degree in pottery will take you where you want to go

Pottery without, not good enough, no matter how good the show

It's all about the degree, the masses agree

Pay that tuition, it will surely set you free

Debt has reached its ceiling there is no turning back

Degrees galore, comprehension continues to lack

The experts will tell you what to do

Walk you through every step until you're thru

Experts, how did they get that way

They paid the tuition, listen to what they say

Blathering heads with degrees, better than you

Scholarships, grants, you know what to do

Negative?

Too much cream in the coffee, torn comforter on the bed

Negative thoughts circling in the head

Sweeten that coffee, comfort from the other side

River rushing, slowly gaining tide

Looking past faults, seeing what lies beyond

We all have a story, favorited different song

Melodies that move you some get stuck in your head

Uplifting, bow breaking, decide instead

There is always a flaw, some negative to fixate on

It's there waiting, dusk to dawn

It's only purpose, to draw away the light

Negative, only if you disagree it's right

Medical

Medical corrupt how dare you say

Corrupt, it's always been that way

Snake oil salesmen selling their ware

Discover something fast, reality too much to bear

Gotta be a better way, you'd think man could do better

Years of science and discovery group think peer letter

Life lived at full pace, medical making the score

Lines at the ER, some going out the door

Natural immunity or as fake as they come

Years of profit costly habit for some

Moving forward will we find a cure

Cost, health, crisis, don't forget to insure

Salesman

A human that sales, male, female doesn't matter

Sales is what sales it's what keep salesmen fatter

Not fat as in fat, fat class, as in better than that

Fat as in comfy, cushy kind of fat

Sale something for something, no worry what

Salesman of the year, grand prized make the cut

Something always for sale take you pick

Drop that cash before it's gone, clickity quick

Salesman always wanting, rarely ever giving back

Drop that call, scamm alert, hackers hack

Gift of gab with a grifters mind

Salesman out selling wasting time earning a dime

Look Away Part?

Look away American it's all just fakes

Shut out distraction whatever it takes

Stay on the marked path, you'll do just fine

Sit back, relax, drink some wine

Too much information floating around today

War rages, close to home, mostly far away

Gas is expensive, food, staples getting hard to find

Getting close to the unemployment line

You get to look away until you can't

Look back, color me rant

Covid started after those Trump years

Things were getting brighter, sparking someone's fears

Look away, miss history as it's being told

Tell you kids about Covid, go ahead be bold

It's not hard to follow, stay focused on the dime

Politics, big money, government grant, taxers dime

You can still be happy and say no to what's going on

Pull the drapes, lights off, different song

Patriots are out there fighting for better times

Going to take getting off those handouts, stopping crime

Government took control for a bit

Freedom to the senses to a big hit

Better days are ahead keep working it through

Better days in America, are up to it voter, it's up to you

Excellence

Raised and trained to strive for excellence

Anything less, makes you petulance

Excellence by whos' standards

Collecting names, passing out lanyards

Excellence, what really does that mean

Some standards of excellence are kind of mean

Perfection, the goal, excellence strives for

Perfection without excellence, kind of a bore

Perfect, however is how we must be

It's best all around, can't you see

The shinning beacon on the hill

Excellence waiting, pay the bill

Day to day trying your best

Excellence out of reach, no time for rest

Can there be excellence yet, no number one

Perfection, excellence, best, nothing left when your done

Exhausting, deep inside says, shouldn't be that way

Could be, other expectations of excellence rule the day

Show your excellence, put your soul into it

Cover every angle, prepare, make it fit

Excellence, the best, perfect in everyway

Excellence until someone differs from your say

Not that one's right or one's even wrong

Different angles of Excellent, critics blasting a song

The critics of excellent always have their say

Smile and walk on, you'll meet another one later today

Sexual Revolution

The hand delt, a losing bet from the start

Women love from the heart, men another part

Free Love became free Sex

Now, free, pay or even text

That's kind of how far we slipped since the revolution began

Not sure which revaluations flamed the biggest fan

Nothing sexy anymore, too much skin, too much shared

New neighbor, not interested, all's been bared

Fashion moves forward, back, somewhere in between

Cover up, there's a lot left to be seen

Mother nature, what must she think

Passing out energy in a wink

Come and take, given away, don't cry

Too much revolution or wings to fly

Women still trying to win the sexual war

Leave them wanting more, exit through the swinging door

Diddle De Notes

Free Energy

Spiritual, sexual, which one do you choose

Too much of either, either way you lose

Hold on tight get ready for a ride

Battles brewing doesn't matter which side

Middle is shattered confusion, regret, maybe lost

One or the other, all agreed at any and all cost

Sinner's sins, saints point out the score

Church lady, Karen, prudent bore

Sinners push farther, how much more can there be

Passing away that energy everything's for free

Behind closed doors, contracts signed, all agree

Nothing much left, not much to see

Balance out, a bit of both works fine

Easing tension, souls lifted, hearts intertwined

Sexual, sensual, religious, spiritual, all of the above

Peace, love, harmony, release the white dove

Too Much Noise

Too much noise, not enough communication

Spinning circles needing a vacation

Worry worry, worry some more

Worries worries, worries galore

Worry about what, can't hear above the noise

Quiet now, says the inner voice

Quiet what, outside or in

Inside is where real conversations begin

Think it through before lashing out

Convinced leave no doubt

Heckling starts not sure which way to turn

Too much noise, alarms blaring, dinner's burned

Not enough Time

Don't have time, enough heard word

Step out of the way, in a hurry, drat, stepped on a turd

Words spoken meant a different way

Words repeated day after day

Need a new meaning for, too much to do

Should not mean, not enough time for you

Still reverberates clinging in the air

To busy, stay put, enter if you dare

Life of being in the way

Run away, hide, return or stay

Not enough time, little soul can't comprehend

Broken hearts left alone to mend

Priorities, make a list

Has consumer life really come to this

Enough time to buy, produce and make

Not enough time, to give God thanks

Not enough time busy every day

Find the time, little souls hear what you say

No more Fun

Stopped being fun, nothing left to say

Run along, busy up that chaotic day

Keep busy, work and work some more

Never wagering a bet, even out the score

Keep everything close, don't give too much

Look at the clock, time for lunch

Betting every morning today, will be it

By lunch time, ya, it's gone to shit

Hunger curbed, back to the square I go

Daily daying, even nightlife is a bore

Opportunities are out there, always is

Stick to the same old same, losing fizz

Brave enough to try, shattered in doubt

Opportunities await, look about

Fight Flight

Flight or fight where do you stand

On your feet, light as a feather, big boxing fan

Opportunity to turn, run or flee

Pinned to the ground, fight or

Groundwork is needed, know where to draw the line

Careful, be aware, penalties, maybe a fine

Join in, look away, stand stooped, face another day

Fight or Flight which game do you play

Careful there, say too much, don't look away

Shoulders back, standing tall, smiling all the day

Living Yin Yang

Living Martial, what does that mean

Sounds kind of scary from what's been seen

Living Martial is balance, awareness, dark and light

Knowing when to observe, flee or fight

Standing ground when the lines been crossed

Chaos happens, in control, still the boss

Boss of self is what we're aiming for

Too many out there trying to settle a score

It's about peace and balance while in the storm

High energy, never slowdown is now the norm

Awareness is lost if you move too fast

Looking back not aware of the past

Martial will pull you into life

Martial teaches war, balances strife

If you can't see conflict how can there be a way

Caught behind closed doors, having no say

Martial as awareness, understanding there's more

Living Martial, a challenging balance act for sure

Big I little i

Big I little i, textbooks say which one i should use

Auto correct suggestion, refused

Big I stands out, small leaves questions behind

Them, me, I, i away we will find

Change the big I to small whenever you can

Small i, big thoughts, humanity, big fan

We will continue forward, it will somehow work out

Big I is about me, little i leaves a little doubt

Once big I is gone, little i will work it thru

Get out there lovelies, we've got diddly work to do

Till we meet again

Except for the virus, divide, corruption, broken boarders, railroads, damaged property lines

After all of that, except, grocery, gas, war, after that, everything seems normally fine

Moving into '24, the seasons and winds keeps changing

Fighting back the flood, the river keeps raging

Smile at your neighbors Lovies, they experienced the same years

Different perspective, loss and suffering, facing different fears

The mend can be mended, we all hope and pray

Stay positive, build for a brighter day

The seasons will come, with each change, something new

Remember, the good in life is from the good you do

About Me

What's there to say?

Wife, mother, grandmother what a bore

Read between the lines, there is always more

Hitting my stride, will get there soon

Wife, mother, grandmother, shooting for the moon

Some things change, most stay the same

Gearing up for the second half, loving life's game

Other Publications: Diddly Do Thru '22
                                  Color Me Diddly

SM

GETTR@ JonnieWall

Truth@jonniewallRHG

X@ JonniewallRHG